What Is Left Behind: Garden Elegies

poems by

Stephanie A. Marcellus

Finishing Line Press
Georgetown, Kentucky

What Is Left Behind: Garden Elegies

Copyright © 2017 by Stephanie A. Marcellus
ISBN 978-1-63534-253-6 First Edition
All rights reserved under International and Pan-American Copyright Conventions.
No part of this book may be reproduced in any manner whatsoever without written permission from the publisher, except in the case of brief quotations embodied in critical articles and reviews.

Publisher: Leah Maines

Editor: Christen Kincaid

Cover Art: Stephanie A. Marcellus

Author Photo: Stephanie A. Marcellus

Cover Design: Elizabeth Maines McCleavy

Printed in the USA on acid-free paper.
Order online: www.finishinglinepress.com
also available on amazon.com

Author inquiries and mail orders:
Finishing Line Press
P. O. Box 1626
Georgetown, Kentucky 40324
U. S. A.

Table of Contents

What Is Left Behind 1

Irises 4

Sweet Violets 6

Marigolds 7

Roses 8

Sweet Rockets 9

Heliotrope 10

Daffodils 12

Ferns 13

Daylilies 14

Pansies 16

*For all those women who came before me,
each passing down their own flowers,
leaving me this garden of words.
For my grandmothers and especially my mother.*

Tread lightly, she is near
Under the snow,
Speak gently, she can hear
The daisies grow.

–Oscar Wilde, "Requiescat"

What Is Left Behind

                  i.
Your gardens to walk through
years after I sang holy, holy,
loyal as a sword of iris
heavy with the scent
of vesper flowers
still thick in my hair.

                  ii.
The hope that you might return
vulnerable again in the skin
with your eyes blue
with your eyes brown.
Your hands as I remember
adorned with silver bands,
and your hands unadorned
but filled with violet petals.

iii.
Signs that you cannot be silenced.
The fires in your roots still burning
in my veins and the dreams of
your crooked thin-lipped smile,
opening like a rosebud to confess
and then your full lips pressed against my ear
soft as a daylily.

iv.
My endeavor to unravel
the delicate stitching
of your sweet violets, pansies,
fern sown along the trellis,
so I can find my way to you
with feverfew bound
tightly to my wrist.

v.

Your marigolds, heliotropes,
gathering in the garden
thick with the scents
of crab apple, sweet rocket.

All these things left behind,
yet still breathing you.

Irises

> *The Greek would often plant an iris on the graves of their beloved women as a tribute to the goddess Iris, whose duty was to take the souls of women to the Elysian fields.*
> –Margaret Grieve, A Modern Herbal

Now, I walk the border
of the garden between
the swords of loyal iris
with shears in my hands
remembering last year's August
how we were shadowed
by this overlook of cedar
thinking ahead to May,
placing the roots in the rich soil.

I stood then with a shovel
and you handed me
the rough-fingered roots gently,
knowing the tubers were tender with life.

We were thinking about the idea
of another spring, picturing bearded petals
with deep purple potential
and lavenders as faint as skyline
inclining to blue rain.

Now, I am writing you a message
with the petals. Inscribing wisdom,
valor, and honor, remembering
how I was barefoot with the earth
drying and tracing the lines in my feet.
You said you used to have feet like mine
with long smooth toes.

Now I place the petals above your brow.
I look down and see my shoes
reflected in headstone's cool granite,
and I try to trace the roots
that creep undetected
beneath the skin.

Sweet Violets
> *Violets, like Primroses, have always been associated with death.*
> –Margaret Grieve, A Modern Herbal

Each spring reawakens
these pale green scions
these runners of your violets and
life lines across my palm and

I wait for you beneath
the heavy blossoms
of the crab apple and

the violet leaves
are heart shaped
veined with green and

each spring I think that your heart
must have been shaped like violet leaves
and might reawaken and

as I wait beneath the heavy scent
of crab apple with a fugue
light in my throat and

the notes become tender stems
of violets that give birth
to themselves against a spring
that is smooth and empty.

Marigolds

> *The Marigold that goes to bed wi' th' sun, and with him rises weeping.*
> —William Shakespeare, The Winter's Tale

Familiar to me—
I tend your marigolds
hardy stems
thick with pungent odor
as September's rich decay
bruises under my thumb.

I think of you,
tending the marigolds
their golden and darkening heads
crimson against the white
stucco of the house.

I tend what is left
careful to avoid
the fragile roots.

I tend,
knowing you
would prefer the crimson
over the gold,
yet knowing nothing more
as my hands catch
on the stems thick
with trickery
against frost, drought
against my knowing
you through the marigolds you left
stationed around the house.

Fragile soldiers left
to protect what is within.

Roses

> *It was once the custom to suspend a Rose over the table as a sign that all confidences were to be held sacred.*
> –Margaret Grieve, A Modern Herbal

Dreamt you
came to me
like rose water
smelling of confession
with the half-light of evening
blooming at your hems,
revealing everything
then nothing—

and I was walking in winter, in a garden
dormant almost inconspicuous
except for rose petals ruddying the snow—
I thought you meant
there was still fire in your roots
thought I should keep this
our secret and gather this thickness,
the waxy red petals between my fingers as an omen—

and I turned
to a rustling
in the woods
I thought you were
coming through
the leaves
thought you were
seeping into
my veins
thought you were
gathering light
at your hems
thought you—

Sweet Rocket
> *In the language of flowers, the Rocket has been taken to represent deceit, since it gives out a lovely perfume in the evening, but in the daytime has none.*
> –Margaret Grieve, A Modern Herbal

So many twilight nights I was lured
into a wooded temple where holiness
seeped from lavender petals into the starred sky.

It was intoxicating.
It was as though
I should close my hands in prayer
as though I might meet you here
as though I might find you mingling
into the cascading dark
or gliding above
this cathedral of pine.

Those woods became a midnight escape.
The elm branches and the pine shoots
seemed taller in the evening's half-light
and the smell of sweet rocket was
thick like whispered vespers,
tying its perfume to everything.

Once I thought I saw
your shadow in the purple haze,
rising over the fern.
Your skirts rushing over downed logs.

I reached for your hand,
but your fingers slipped from my grasp
like the sweet rocket's scent on the dawn's wind,
leaving me behind
choking on the sweet rocket's dying breath.
Its scent evaporating as the sky
became more sun than shadow.

Everywhere, there is nothing left of you.

Heliotrope

> *Heliotrope means shunned by the sun. The Greek word heliotrope means to turn towards the sun.*
> –Margaret Grieve, A Modern Herbal

Can I ever forgive
you for parting
your leaves, turning
your edges sunward
shedding the human
skin like a milkweed
pod come undone—
the roughly hewn
corporeal form merely
a chariot for the seed
that scatters in airy rapture
and leaves
me here shadowed
by the trailing light
of your sudden departure
leaves me
heavy with skin
thick with blood
rootless in your garden
with free will
to seek out another
orchard or meadow
but where
can I possibly escape
this anger
at your cells
at my internal landscape
where I could find myself
so easily lost
in the mysterious
flowerings of organs

a captive
in my own body
caught in the current
of veins
snagged between
the branches
of capillaries
tendriling against the tissue?

I am alone
untangling the vines.

Daffodils

> *The name, narcissus, comes from a Greek word meaning to numb.*
> –Margaret Grieve, A Modern Herbal

Out the window, the daffodil bulbs
you planted in the fall
have forced
their green stems through the thawing soil

I write: *Can almost feel the petals fall across my face.*
Last fall I felt so optimistic.

The daffodils are bending to catch
their reflections
in the leftover snow.
They are caught
somewhere between spring and winter.

I write: *This morning I wanted to walk into the garden*
and be numbed by the fragrance.

Now the dawn edges its gray light
onto the too smooth
sheets of the bed.
Your stationery feels starchy
beneath my hands.

I write: *I must be caught somewhere between—*
The raw edges of spring are pushing up against my soil.

The ink in my pen is difficult:
a scratchy voice for my tight throat.

Ferns

> *It is believed that treading on a fern will cause the poor unfortunate traveler to become confused and lose his way.*
> –Margaret Grieve, A Modern Herbal

And if I should lose myself
among the fern
what I mean to say
is that I am
canopied
by blue sky
or that I am
captured
between the roots of the elm
or maybe I mean
encircled
with fronds or is it
ensnared
in their lacework
or perhaps I mean that
I will find myself—
such a strange relief—to be
invisible
or maybe just
unseen
in this forest

a green tendril
an edge of bracken
a leaf
that cannot hear
its name
called from afar

Daylilies

> *The Chinese called the daylily "husan t'sao" meaning "the plant of forgetfulness" as it was supposed to allay sorrow by causing forgetfulness.*
> –Margaret Grieve, A Modern Herbal

I like to remember myself
walking down to the creek
with you on a July morning.
We were carefully navigating
our way among the cattails,
through the spongy lowland bogs.
I carried the bucket.
You held the shovel like a walking stick.

We talked about nothing
in particular. Our destination:
the tangerine and gold speckles
we had glimpsed from the road.
As we neared the lilies,
they became more than ghost lanterns,
bobbing their heads over the cattails.

The sun was heavy on our backs.
We rolled up our sleeves
to reveal our arms similarly freckled,
and together we dug and gathered
the roots and damp soil of the lilies
and put them into the bucket
to transplant at home.

Somehow deep down I knew
that this would be our last walk
when you told me that daylilies would
cause us to forget our sorrows.
I knew that we were taking our own cure from the earth.

I like to imagine that someday
when I am as old as you were then
that I will walk along the edges
of the creek's banks with my daughters, my granddaughters
and we will search again
among the serpentine leaves
for the rusted orange and yellow lilies.

We will let them murmur soothing nothings
into our ears from their swan-like throats.

Forgetfulness will be lovely and deep.

Pansies
> *And there is pansies, that's for thoughts.*
> –*William Shakespeare,* Hamlet

Stutter stuttering petal petals
on my tongue stinging nettles—this
is me coming through the rushes—my skirts
heavy, weeping willow for hair, moss
rooted on my feet—falter, faltering
roses in my mouth—confessing desire
for honey bees, sun, prickling needles of yew.

Not leaving—I have not left
yet—language returning slowly—violets
in my throat—pain, pander, *pense* (to think)
I could be hopeful—greedy seed catalog
in January—seasons ahead in thought—
panther-faced pansies—I am wearing
your face in my veins: *Baby Lucia* (sky blue,
cold tolerant), *Blues Jam* (blue shades and
bicolors), *Crystal Bowls* (nine colors, early,
many flower, heat tolerant), *Fama See Me*
(purple edge and blotch with white between),
Padparadja (intense orange, named for orange
sapphire), *Queen of the Planets* (early, large
dark blotches), *Spanish Sun* (tangerine orange),
Ullswater Blue (gentian blue, black blotch) of

—my feet spilling spilled out—the blooms
and roots—green stalks eyelashes and nerves—faces
you said in a pansy—I could find—heavy
too heavy for the stem—once you told me this—
but I am tangled untangling creeper vine—
I am outside the garden looking beyond.

Stephanie A. Marcellus is an associate professor at Wayne State College where she teaches creative writing and literature. She holds an MFA from Colorado State University and a PhD from The University of South Dakota. Her work has appeared or is forthcoming in *Plainsongs, Three Drops from a Cauldron, Alligator Juniper* among others.

www.ingramcontent.com/pod-product-compliance
Lightning Source LLC
LaVergne TN
LVHW041526070426
835507LV00013B/1840